Finding Freedom

An Eight-Week Journey Recapturing Your Identity,
Faith, and Body Image

Alyssa Bethke and Sadie Robertson
with Elizabeth Hyndman

Published by Jefferson & Alyssa Bethke. Titles may be purchased in bulk for educational, business, fund-raising, or sales promotional use. For more information please email help@jeffandalyssa.com.

All Scripture from The Christian Standard Bible. Copyright © 2017 by Holman Bible Publishers. Used by permission. Christian Standard Bible®, and CSB® are federally registered trademarks of Holman Bible Publishers, all rights reserved.

www.zondervan.com.

The FINDING*balance*® "bird" logo and "Next Right Steps" content appears courtesy of FINDING*balance*, Inc. © 2018. All rights reserved. May not be reproduced without permission.

The Library of Congress Cataloging-in-Publication Data is on file with the Library of Congress
ISBN-13: 978-1-7342746-6-0

What is a workbook without videos?

This workbook follows along with eight videos created by Alyssa and Sadie. Please send a copy of your receipt for the workbook to findingfreedom@jeffandalyssa.com and we will send you a link to access the video series. If you have any trouble with this contact support@jeffandalyssa.com

If you would like to purchase additional copies of the workbook. This only applies if you have purchased the video series already. The cost is $19.99 findingfreedomworkshop.com/extraworkbooks

Thanks,
Alyssa and Sadie

If you would like to check out some of our t-shirts, posters, prints and other goodies head over to:

www.findingfreedomworkshop.com

Use the code FREEDOMFOUND for $10 off any Finding Freedom merchandise or gifts.

Finding Freedom

Table of Contents

Introduction

Friend,

We are so glad you are here! If you are like us, you know what it's like to feel trapped, to feel unloved, and to feel insecure. If that is you, you are in the right place! We have all felt that way at some point, but by God's grace, we have found freedom. We want to show you how you can find freedom, too!

In this Bible study, we're going to go all the way back to the beginning of time. It may seem weird at first, but we have to start there because that is where everything starts. Together, we'll discover how our Creator made us and delights in us and how He sent His Son to die for us, just the way we are. We'll see how we are all broken, but also how we can be made whole and new. We'll learn how we can change and grow and how we can find true freedom in Christ. We'll explore what it really means to love ourselves and how to give God glory in serving and loving those made in His image.

We can't wait to walk this journey with you. Let's find freedom in Christ, together.

We've provided some short "Video Time" pages at the beginning of every week. If you are doing this study by yourself, you can just skip the opening review and discussion questions and answer the video teaching questions in your journal. You are not alone in this journey!

If you are doing this study with a group, use the Video Time pages as a template for your group time together. Those pages are there if you need them, but you know your group the best. Feel free to adjust as needed.

Lastly, if you watch the videos you will see just the two of us--Sadie and Alyssa. But this project also wouldn't be what it is without the help of the incredible Elizabeth Hyndman. She's responsible for the incredible journey through the Scriptures you're about to go through in the coming weeks, so we wanted to make sure you knew all three of us as you walk this path toward freedom!

One note before we begin: If you are struggling with your body or with food, please consult a medical doctor and a biblical, Christian counselor before beginning any changes with your diet and exercise. We truly believe God can heal you. And as agents of this healing process He has given us doctors, nutritionists, trainers, and counselors to help us change the way we take care of our bodies in a healthy way.

We also recommend connecting with our ministry partner FINDINGbalance®. You will find helpful tips from them throughout this study wherever you see this little icon. They have also created a special support page for you at www.findingbalance.com/freedom.

Week 1

VIDEO TIME

GET TO KNOW ONE ANOTHER!

1. What drew you to this study?

....

2. What do you hope to gain from our time together?

....

3. If you could vacation anywhere in the world—money doesn't matter—where would you go?

....

WATCH THE VIDEO TEACHING FOR WEEK 1.

VIDEO QUESTIONS:

1. How would you define "freedom"?

....

2. What encouraged you from Alyssa's and Sadie's stories?

....

3. Have you yet hit a point of saying "no more" to something? If so, share a little about that situation
    with the group.

....

....

DAYS 1 & 2

Your Story

T his study is an extremely personal study. Every person's struggle is a little bit different. Every person's victory is a little bit different. Every person's story will be different, too.

This first week, we're going to spend some time journaling our stories, similar to how Alyssa and Sadie shared theirs in the opening video. We won't have as much study this week, but I encourage you to take your time, praying as you write.

READ JOSHUA 4:1-9.

Why did Joshua tell the men to carry the stones?

....

....

In verse 7, what are the people to tell their children when they ask about the stones?

....

....

This story takes place after the people crossed the Jordan River on dry land. They placed the stones to re-mind themselves and their children and all the generations after them that God provides. They said, "Right here, in this place, God cared for His people."

Take time to write down your story. Start with when you were born and go up until now. As you write out your story, note all the times God has cared for you, if you know of any. Set your story out like the stones, to remind you of what He has done in your life. If you don't know of any times yet, that's okay. We're praying this study will be one such stone for you.

....

....

....

DAYS 3 & 4

Freedom

L ook over the story you wrote yesterday. Take a different color pen or highlighter and underline all the places and times you felt trapped, burdened, or not-free.

Next take a different color pen or highlighter and mark all the places you felt freedom, even just a little taste of it.

Pray, thanking God for all the times you have felt free in Him. Ask Him to help you be free in who He is and who He has made you to be. Pray for your friends in this study with you—even if you are studying by yourself and don't know the names of other women around the world who may be studying about God's freedom with you.

READ GALATIANS 1:11-24.

Whose story is this?

....

....

Write verse 24 below:

....

....

Friend, your story can be used by God, too. No matter how many times you marked that you felt trapped or burdened or alone, He can change your story. He can set you free. And He can use your story of finding freedom to bring Himself glory!

This week's Next Right Step from our friends at FINDING*balance*®:

Head over to <u>www.findingbalance.com</u> and take their free "eating issues" self-test.

Week 2

VIDEO TIME

REVIEW QUESTIONS:

1. Ask a few group members to share their stories, or an abbreviated version. (Group leaders: be prepared to share your own story if no one else is comfortable doing so.)

2. How can we pray for you this week?

WATCH THE VIDEO TEACHING FOR WEEK 2.

VIDEO QUESTIONS:

1. Have you told someone in your life (outside of this group) about your struggle to find freedom from food and body image issues?

2. Read Psalm 146:7-8 as a group. Which phrase in this verse most encourages you? Which one do you have the hardest time believing is true?

3. Pray for one another, that God will bring boldness to walk toward His light and abundance.

DAY 1

We are the Pinnacle of Creation

In the video this week, Alyssa and Sadie talked about how dark it is to live believing the lies of the enemy. The darkness makes us feel alone and the lies seem personal, but we will see this week how God has brought light and truth into our lives from the very beginning.

"In the beginning ..."

The story of the world, the story of humans, the story of you, begins with those three words. They are the "once upon a time" of our true story.

READ GENESIS 1:1-3.

What existed before God?

....

....

How did God create light?

....

....

In the beginning God spoke our world into existence. He said, "Let there be light." And there it was. He created the sky, the sea, and the land. He created evening and morning.

On the third day of creation, we get another small glimpse into the character of our Creator.

READ GENESIS 1:9-13.

What additional fact is added to this third day of creation? Hint: You can find it at the end of verses 10 and 12.

....

....

....

Not only did God create everything out of nothing, He made it good. He is a good Creator. He made sunflowers and oak trees. He made avocados, lemons, tomatoes, and peppers. (Guacamole, anyone?) God spoke it all into existence and then He saw that it was good.

After that, He made stars, seasons, and sunrises and sunsets. He made the moon. Then, He filled the seas with fish and whales and sharks and shrimp. He filled the sky with birds. He saw that they were good and He gave them a job.

Write God's directions in Genesis 1:22 to the birds and the fish:

....

....

God saw that they were good. He then turned His attention to the aardvarks and zebras, beetles, camels, chipmunks, and tigers. God saw that they were good.

READ GENESIS 1:26-28.

When you think about the word *image,* what comes to mind?

....

....

How would you define the word *image?* Break out a dictionary (or a dictionary app) if you need to!

....

....

An image depicts something else. An image of a coffee cup depicts the coffee cup in my Instagram feed. It isn't actual coffee—I can't drink a photo of a cup—but it represents coffee.

In many cases, an *image* is a replica. It means "the same as" or "very similar to." Human beings are not God, but we are made in His image.

What do you think it means to be made in God's image?

....

....

Being made in God's image means we are similar to Him. We represent Him on earth. We reflect God. We're imperfect representatives and reflections, though. We're not the exact same as Him, but we point to what He is like.

Does remembering that we are God's images cause you to reconsider how you think about and treat other people? In what ways?

....

....

Does it cause you to think differently about yourself? How so?

....

....

In Genesis 1:27, God breaks out into poetry. Has that ever happened to you? Maybe not, but have you ever been so happy you've burst into song? A similar thing happens in another telling of this same story.

The Creator God, maker of peacocks and elephants and clownfish, roses, magnolia trees, and constellations spoke poetry over human beings. We are the pinnacle of creation.

Turn to Isaiah 43 and read verses 1 through 7. Why did God create humans?

....

....

God didn't create us because He needed us. He created us for His glory and we are precious in His sight. You are precious to Him. Poetry has been written about how you were formed.

Now let's continue to Genesis 2, which gives a short recap of the creation of the world, and then zooms in on the creation of human beings.

READ GENESIS 2:7,18-23.

From these verses and Genesis 1:26-31, fill in the chart below with the differences between the creation of animals and the creation of human beings.

	Animals	Humans
Mode of creation	Spoken into existence	
Command from God	"Be fruitful, multiply, and fill the waters of the seas, and let the birds multiply on the earth." v. 22	
God saw that it was ...	Good	

God made man in His own image by literally breathing life into his lungs. God loved the man and gave him everything he needed. He gave the man a job—to name all the animals. While the man was giving every animal a name, he was looking for a helper fit for him. He was looking for a companion, one like him. He was looking for someone to be in community with, to know, to explore creation with.

None of the animals fit the bill. So God created a woman and brought her to the man. The man exclaimed, *Here is one like me!* And he broke out into poetry.

Look at the poems in Genesis 1:27 and Genesis 2:23. Do you notice a similarity? What is it?

....

....

Both of these poems say, *This one is like me.* As creatures created in the image of God, we were made like Him. On the evening of the sixth day, after looking at all He had created, God said that it was "very good indeed" (1:31).

From that point on, all humans bore and bear the image of God. Another image bearer, years later, wrote another poem about the pinnacle of God's creation—humans.

READ PSALM 139:13-16.

You may have heard this poem before. It is a psalm of David, a man after God's own heart (1 Samuel 13:14). David was also a man who had an affair and sent the woman's husband to war to be killed. He wasn't perfect by any means, but he was "remarkably and wondrously made" (Psalm 139:14).

These lines of poetry continue the theme of those in Genesis. This time, though, David is praising God, His Creator, with lines that say, *Thank You for making me like You.*

Let's end today by writing our own poems of praise to God. They don't have to rhyme, and I promise I won't ask you to show them to anyone.

Praise God
for making you
remarkably,
wondrously, and
like Him.

DAY 2

When Sin and Shame Enter

We all wish we could just end the Bible and this study at the end of yesterday, in awe of our Creator and in celebration of being His very good creations. We love the sweet story of God creating trout and toads and tiger lilies. We love the poetry of being made in His image.

God created man and woman and placed them in paradise—a garden called Eden. He gave them the job of ruling over the animals and the land, of being fruitful and multiplying. He gave them beautiful trees and trees bearing delicious fruit. The man worked the land, but he did not toil. The man and the woman walked with God in the garden.

READ GENESIS 2:25 AND WRITE IT BELOW.

Why do you think the man and the woman felt no shame, despite the fact that they were naked?

....

....

The man and the woman were made perfectly in a perfect place. They didn't feel shame because shame didn't exist. They were completely naked, exposed, vulnerable. Yet they were not ashamed. Their exposure and vulnerability met safety and security in the perfect place with God who made them.

Then everything changed.

READ GENESIS 2:16-17.

What command did God give the man?

....

....

The first words God gives the man in the command are, "You are free." He doesn't begin with restrictions. In fact, He has given the man and the woman all the trees in the garden to eat from, except one. They are to stay away from the one tree. If they eat from it, they will "certainly die."

You may be familiar with this story. You may have seen it depicted in cartoons and in Sunday School coloring pages and read it in several versions. Today as you read it, try to think about the life before this moment. Think about the freedom, the vulnerability, of being exposed and unashamed. Think about the love and joy of walking with God in paradise day after day.

NOW READ GENESIS 3:1-7. Rewrite the story in your own words. Don't forget verse 7 in light of Genesis 2:25.

....

....

....

Yesterday we read the origin story of our world and everything in it. Just now we read the origin story of sin, of shame, and of looking at ourselves and thinking, "This is not good."

Sin, put simply, is disobeying God. The man and the woman disobeyed God's clear instructions not to eat from the tree of good and evil. Despite everything they were free to do and be, they did the one thing that was prohibited.

We continue to disobey God, to sin, whenever we ignore a command for us written in His Word, whenever we say no to things He has said we should do, and whenever we say yes to those things He has forbidden. The man and the woman were the first creations, the first image bearers of God. They were also the first to disobey Him.

The first consequence of their disobedience is revealed in verse 7. Their eyes were opened and "they knew they were naked." They realized for the first time that they were exposed, that they were vulnerable. They immediately attempted to cover up.

Has there been a time in your life when you felt suddenly exposed for something?

....

....

....

I have many instances of this in my own life, but I remember clearly a time when I was little and slapped my younger sister across the face. I don't remember my motives. I don't know if she had said something that annoyed me or took something from me or if I was just in a bad mood. But I slapped her and she cried. We were the only two in the room. My handprint burned red on her stung skin. I couldn't hide.

My mom came into the room and looked at my sister who told her the truth, that I had slapped her. I don't remember if I had any sort of defense, but my mom looked at me and asked, "Is this true?"

READ GENESIS 3:8-13. List the questions God asked the man and the woman below.

1.
....

2.
....

3.
....

4.
....

Flip back to Psalm 139 and read verses 1-6. What do these verses tell you about God?

....

....

God knows everything. To use a fancy term, He is omniscient. He knows when we sleep and when we're awake. He knows what we're going to say before we even say it.

Knowing that God knows everything, why do you think He asked the man and the woman these questions?

....

....

When I slapped my sister and stood by as she told my mom what happened, I was obviously guilty. No need to brush for fingerprints or call witnesses to the stand. The case was closed before it was even opened.

Yet my mom asked me if I did it. She gave me a chance to admit my guilt before deciding on a punishment.

I wonder if God gave the man and the woman the same opportunity. He knew where they were, how they realized they were naked, that they ate from the forbidden tree, and what, specifically, the woman did in the process. He didn't ask to find out the answer for Himself. Perhaps He asked so that they would have the opportunity to confess. Perhaps He asked so that they would understand the answers themselves.

Let's look at the rest of the consequences of their actions. READ GENESIS 3:14-19.

List the consequences for each party involved below.

•	•	•
•	•	•
•	•	•
•	•	•
Serpent	**Woman**	**Man**

In verse 20, the woman gets a name—Eve. *Eve* means *living* or *life*.
Her name comes attached to a promise.

READ VERSE 15 AGAIN. What is the promise to Eve in this verse?

....

....

Here, in the middle of giving out necessary consequences, God also gives a promise. He promises that Eve's offspring will one day crush the head of the serpent. Here, after everything perfect was broken, we are given hope.

READ GENESIS 3:22-24 TO SEE THE REST OF THE CONSEQUENCES FOR THE FIRST SIN.

While human beings were created in God's image, we were not created to be exactly like Him. We are His image bearers, but we are not God. In verse 22, God reveals one way we were not created like Him. Once we had the knowledge of good and evil we were no longer allowed to partake of the tree of life. We were kicked out of paradise.

But we still have the promise, the promise of hope.

DAY 3

Hope in Christ

In paradise, the man, Adam, and Eve walked with God. Literally. Genesis 3:8 says they "heard the sound of the LORD God walking in the garden." We don't know exactly what this looked like or meant, but we know it signifies an intimate relationship with God.

They knew God. They talked with Him. They walked, fully exposed, with Him. Paradise was their home with Him.

When they disobeyed God by eating of the one forbidden tree, they did not instantly die. Instead, they were separated from the tree of life and separated from God.

But God promised. He promised that one day One would come who would crush the serpent's head. Then He clothed Adam and Eve. He killed an animal and covered them with fur. He covered up their shame, their vulnerability, their nakedness.

READ 1 CORINTHIANS 15:21-22. Fill in the blanks below:

Since _____ came through a man, the _____ also comes through a man.

For just as in _____ all die, so also in _____ all will be made alive.

Because we are humans, we are image bearers of God, but we also have inherited the sin of Adam, meaning we are sinful. None of us are exempt from disobedience to God.

Read the following verses and sum each one up in your own words.

Romans 3:23

....

....

Romans 6:2

....

....

Ephesians 2:8-9

....

....

2 Corinthians 5:21

....

....

Romans 10:9-10

....

....

Those verses may be familiar to you, but don't miss the promise and the promise fulfilled in their words. What do these verses mean for us humans?

....

....

Thousands of years after man first sinned and God sacrificed animals to cover their nakedness, He sent His Son to die for our sins, covering us in His righteousness. Nothing—I repeat, nothing—we do can earn us this righteousness, wholeness. God gives us His righteousness, covering our sins, as a gift.

We just have to accept the gift.

It sounds simple and it is, but it is not easy. God sent His Son, Jesus, to die for us. Like the animals God sacrificed in Genesis 3, Jesus' blood covers our sin and shame.

READ ROMANS 4:20-25. What will be credited to us if we believe?

....

....

FINDING FREEDOM · WORKBOOK

Accepting the gift of life with God also means letting go of our old selves. Instead of playing by our rules and serving ourselves, we serve God and submit to His authority in our lives. We admit we cannot serve Him, obey Him, and submit to Him on our own and we repent of trying. We repent of our disobedience, turning away from sin and self and to God and forgiveness. We respond to His gift by confessing with our mouths and believing with our hearts (Romans 10:9-10). Then we are saved to a life with Him forever.

Maybe you've already accepted the free gift of grace offered by God through His Son. If so, spend some time thanking God for life with Him. Pray for those you know who have not yet made the decision to follow Him.

Maybe you have never known what it took to be with God forever. Maybe you didn't know how simple it can be to accept His gift of grace. Maybe you want to do that right now. If so, talk to God, admitting you have disobeyed Him, asking for help, and confessing Jesus as your Savior—the One who died for your sins. Ask Him to be the Lord of your life. Thank Him for the gift of salvation and life with Him forever.

If you made the decision to follow Christ for the first time, or if you still have questions about this whole process, please ask someone you know who is following Jesus. They would love to help you!

You may be wondering what all of this has to do with freedom from food. We cannot have freedom apart from Christ. We cannot know who we are without first knowing Him.

In Acts 15, Paul argues on behalf of the Gentiles (non-Jewish people) that Christ alone is needed for salvation. The Christ followers who were also Jews tried to impose upon new believers Jewish laws and regulations in order to be saved. They argued Jesus plus the Law equalled salvation.

READ WHAT PAUL SAYS ABOUT THIS EQUATION IN VERSES 7-11.

What have you tried to put into the equation for salvation in the past? Fill in the blank below.

Jesus + _____ = salvation

Paul argued that Jesus plus nothing equals salvation. We are saved through the grace of Jesus Christ. Nothing more, nothing less.

In Galatians, this topic comes up again.

READ GALATIANS 5:1. Who set us free?

....

....

What do you think the "yoke of slavery" was?

....

....

The Jewish laws and regulations are referred to as a "yoke" a few times in the Bible. A yoke is a wooden piece that is attached to machinery and worn by farm animals across the neck or shoulder. This is how they might pull a plow through soil to till it. Essentially, it was a heavy burden. Paul is asking the new believers to stand firm in the freedom of Christ, who fulfilled every law, and to not take up again the burden of trying to be perfect.

Christ set us free from the burden of perfection. He set us free from sin. He set us free from shame. In Him, we find freedom.

DAY 4

Journal

E ach week, we'll spend one day journaling, or writing down what
God is teaching us through His Word. You can use this space for
prayer and reflection. We'll have a few prompts to help you get
started, but there are no rules here!

What I learned about God through the Bible this week:

....

....

....

....

What I learned about myself from Scripture this week:

....

....

....

....

How I should respond in obedience to what I am learning:

....

....

....

....

Prayer requests:

....

....

....

....

....

Three specific things I'm thankful for this week:

1.

....

2.

....

3.

....

This week's Next Right Step from our friends at FINDING*balance*®:

Consider one way food issues are stealing from you. Write it here:

....

....

....

....

Week 3

VIDEO TIME

REVIEW QUESTIONS:

1. When you think about the word *image*, what comes to mind?

    ....

2. Does remembering that we are God's images cause you to reconsider how you think about and treat other people? In what ways?

    ....

3. Why do you think the man and the woman felt no shame, despite the fact that they were naked?

    ....

4. Knowing that God knows everything, why do you think He asked the man and the woman questions in Genesis 3?

    ....

5. If you're comfortable sharing, discuss what you put in the blank in the Jesus + _____ = salvation equation.

WATCH THE VIDEO TEACHING.

VIDEO QUESTIONS:

1. What have you had to get rid of (or what do you want the courage to get rid of) in order to start to live in more freedom?

    ....

....

....

....

2. Read Joshua 6:1-20 together. Spend time in prayer praising God for the victory He is leading you
    toward.

....

....

....

3. Does it empower you or discourage you to know that your current struggles are part of a spiritual
    war (Ephesians 6:12) with a battle taking place in your mind? How so?

....

....

....

....

....

....

4. Pair up and ask God to open your ears and the ears of your partner to hear what God says about you.

....

....

....

....

....

....

This week's Next Right Step from our friends at FINDING*balance*®:

Make a list of 2-3 people you have in your life right now that you can be honest with.

1.
....

2.
....

3.
....

DAY 1

New Creations

"New Year, New You."

I love New Year resolutions. Mine rarely last an entire year, but I love the thought of reinventing myself—or at least reinventing a few habits—as the calendar rolls around to January 1 each year. Whether you make resolutions on January 1 or you decide to make a change on March 24 or September 18, we all love the idea of starting over, doing things differently this time.

Instead of "new year, new you," Paul often preached a "new life, new you" message. When we become followers of Jesus, accepting His gracious gift of life with God forever, we become new people. We are new creations. Out with the old, in with the new!

READ EPHESIANS 4:20-24. In this passage, Paul lists a three-step process for change. What are the three steps?

1.

....

2.

....

3.

....

This process is mentioned throughout Scripture. We see it in the life of Paul himself. Once we are believers, we are declared righteous immediately by God. We are covered by the righteousness of Jesus. We call that justification. We are justified by faith in Christ.

Second Corinthians 5:17 says, "Therefore, if anyone is in Christ, he is a new creation; the old has passed away, and see, the new has come!"

What do you think it means to be a new creation?

....

....

As new creations, we can't stop there. We, like Adam and Eve, are to be fruitful and multiply. We are to bear the fruit of the Spirit and make disciples.

What are the fruit of the Spirit? READ GALATIANS 5:22-23 AND LIST THEM BELOW.

1.

....

2.

....

3.

....

4.

....

5.

....

6.

....

7.

....

8.

....

9.

....

Which of these are easiest for you to exhibit? Which are the most difficult?

....

....

....

....

....

Our lives as believers should be marked by all of those qualities. Bearing this fruit and making disciples, stumbling in our efforts, repenting, and trying again is a process called sanctification. Paul says, "work out your own salvation with fear and trembling" (Philippians 2:12b). That doesn't mean we're supposed to live our days in fear, but to walk in holy reverence of God's work in our lives. His grace is always available to us, but we should not take lightly that we are new creations.

TURN BACK TO EPHESIANS 4:20-24. What is the new self, according to verse 24?

....

....

There's that hint of God's image again. The new self was made in God's likeness in righteousness and purity of the truth. If you are in Christ, this is who you are!

The other verses in this section outline the three-step process toward change. A "three-step process" sounds easy, right? Well, let's take a closer look.

Step 1: Take off your former way of life (v. 22).

We are to take off our former way of life, our sins, our shame, our disobedience.

My junior year of college, we had an event called Midnight Mudness. It was tradition that all the juniors would all put on old clothes and go out to a field on campus at midnight. The event team had prepared the field by hosing it down with fire hoses to create mud. Our campus was generally pretty muddy, so it probably didn't take long to get a good mud pit going. We played games in the mud for about an hour until we were completely covered in mud. I have before and after pictures and some of us are difficult to identify beneath the layer of dirt and mud.

Imagine if we'd gone into our dorms, taken off our muddy clothes and just put on clean clothes without showering or washing off. Gross, right?

Let's think of our former way of life as those muddy clothes. We need to take off our former way of life.

How do we take off our former way of life?

....

....

I hate to say it, but this is where things get difficult. We take off our former way of life by repenting. The easiest way to think about repentance is to think of a U-turn. You're headed toward sin (former way of life) but then you realize what you are doing, you stop, turn around, and head away from it.

When we take off our former way of life, that means we stop disobeying and repent. We begin to head in the opposite direction. Of course this is easier said than done. Which leads us to step two of the change process.

Step 2: Be renewed in the spirit of your minds (v. 23).

If we were to take off our former life and stop there, it would be like the junior class, mud-covered, not even trying to wash off the mud before trying to continue our lives. We stopped playing in the mud, but we're still muddy until we move on to step two.

How are we renewed in the spirit of our minds?

....

....

....

We will talk about this more next week, but for now know that renewing your mind is a necessary part of the process.

When we were all muddy and gross, we didn't want to touch anything clean. We decided to try to rinse off as much as possible in the yard before heading back into our dorm rooms. We really only had a couple of sources of water—two garden hoses run from the common rooms. Several of us tried to share a hose, taking turns rinsing off as much mud as possible.

While waiting my turn with the water, I turned around to see my friend Andy rinsing off in a puddle. He was splashing his face with water that wasn't much cleaner than what he was rinsing off. When I asked what he was doing, he realized he was essentially washing off mud with muddy water. We were giddy already from the adrenaline of mud games at midnight and when we all saw what was happening, we laughed until we cried.

The truth is, we often try to do what Andy was doing. We try to take off our old sins and wash them off with things that are not really clean. Instead of getting drunk to numb our pain, we eat too much. Instead of eating too much, we abuse our bodies. Instead of abusing our bodies, we worry incessantly. We keep trying to put the former way of life back on.

Instead, we are to go to step three.

Step 3: Put on the new self (v. 24).

The only way to really clean up after midnight mudness was to take off our old muddy clothes, get in the shower and completely clean off, and then to put on clean clothes.

How do you put on the new self?

....

....

....

Paul doesn't leave us in the hypothetical here. He gives us some clear examples of things to take off and things to put on in the next section.

Read the verses below, putting squares around the things we must take off and circling the things we must put on.

Therefore, putting away lying, speak the truth, each one to his neighbor, because we are members of one another. 26 Be angry and do not sin. Don't let the sun go down on your anger, 27 and don't give the devil an opportunity. 28 Let the thief no longer steal. Instead, he is to do honest work with his own hands, so that he has something to share with anyone in need. 29 No foul language should come from your mouth, but only what is good for building up someone in need, so that it gives grace to those who hear. 30 And don't grieve God's Holy Spirit. You were sealed by him for the day of redemption. 31 Let all bitterness, anger and wrath, shouting and slander be removed from you, along with all malice. 32 And be kind and compassionate to one another, forgiving one another, just as God also forgave you in Christ.
Ephesians 4:25-32

What did you notice about the pairings of things we must put off and those we must put on?

....

....

....

....

We don't exchange our former ways of life for things that resemble our former ways of life. We put on the opposite of what we take off. We put away lying and put on speaking the truth. We put away stealing and put on working and sharing. We put off foul language and put on language that builds others up.

In this way, we are changed. Out with the old, in with the new! Three steps makes us think the process is easy, but I can testify it is not. We often really like our former ways of life. We're comfortable in our mud-soaked clothes. Plus, it takes work to clean up, to put on clean clothes. We'll fail a lot. In fact, we'll fail every time we try to do it ourselves.

Take heart, though, because God has given us the Holy Spirit to help. Philippians 2:13 says God works in us to will and to work according to His good purpose. He will work in you, too. And this three-step process, like most things, gets easier with practice.

End today by praying the prayer Paul prayed in Ephesians 3:14-21:

For this reason I kneel before the Father 15 from whom every family in heaven and on earth is named. 16 I pray that he may grant you, according to the riches of his glory, to be strengthened with power in your inner being through his Spirit, 17 and that Christ may dwell in your hearts through faith. I pray that you, being rooted and firmly established in love, 18 may be able to comprehend with all the saints what is the length and width, height and depth of God's love, 19 and to know Christ's love that surpasses knowledge, so that you may be filled with all the fullness of God.

20 Now to him who is able to do above and beyond all that we ask or think according to the power that works in us— 21 to him be glory in the church and in Christ Jesus to all generations, forever and ever. Amen.

DAY 2

The Way Out

Many times in my life I've thought I was the only one. I was the only one to be betrayed by my friends that way. I was the only one to worry all night long. I was the only one still single. I was the only one with this illness, who looked like that, who felt this way.

I'm sure you've also had your "only one" moments. Yours may be completely different than mine, or they may overlap a little, because, as I've discovered, we're never the only ones. While the exact circumstances of our lives don't repeat in the lives of others, we more often hear ourselves say "me too" than "I've never ..." This is true of our circumstances, our feelings, and our thoughts, as well as our temptations and sins.

READ 1 CORINTHIANS 10:13. What does this tell us about our temptations?

....

....

....

I don't know about you, but this verse brings me great comfort. I'm not the only one! It says that I've experienced no temptation that is uncommon or unique. It may feel unique to me, but I can be assured that others have felt this same temptation. Some have fallen to their temptations and committed the sin, but some have persevered through the temptation, renewing their minds, putting on godly things. There is hope.

What does this verse tell us about God?

....

....

....

God is faithful. He stays true to His promises and right here He promises to always offer a way out. We never have to sin. No matter how hopeless the situation is, no matter how impossible it seems, we can stand firm.

NOW FLIP TO HEBREWS 4:14-16. Who is our high priest?

....

....

Why is Christ able to sympathize with our weaknesses? What does this passage tell you about Jesus?

....

....

....

....

I love verse 16, "Therefore ..." Because Jesus is our high priest who understands our weaknesses because He has been there before, in light of that astounding news, we can approach the throne with boldness. We can approach the throne of the One who has "passed through the heavens" (v. 15) because His throne is one of grace. His throne is one of sympathy, where we find mercy and grace in our time of need.

We are not the only ones. And we serve a God who sent His Son to live with us, to be tempted in every way that we are, but who paved the way out without sin. He is one of the not-the-only-ones with us. He says, "Me too. I understand."

Take a moment right now to stop and praise God for Jesus, our high priest who sympathizes with our weaknesses. Pray, thanking Him for His grace and mercy. If you need to confess unadmitted sin, do so now, too, knowing you can approach His throne with boldness.

Something unusual happens when we understand that we all struggle, that we all have temptations that are "common to mankind." We become more open with others. If I know you've been there, I feel no shame in telling you I've been there, too.

Our temptations are not always exactly the same. I may run back to worrying and anxiety as my default, and someone else might run to sex or pornography, another runs to please other people, while still someone else runs to food or away from food. We are all constantly going through the put off, renew, put on process. And sometimes, if we're honest, we're caught washing mud off with muddy water.

The good news is we're not alone in the puddles and we don't have to stay there. Not only does Jesus understand what we're going through, He's offered us a way out.

Flip back to 1 Corinthians 10 and read verse 14. What is the first word in the verse?

....

Your translation may say "Therefore" or "So then." This is a signal, just like in Hebrews 4:16, to look back at the previous context. Because of what just happened, do this. Because of the truth in verse 13 that no temptation has overtaken us but that which is common to mankind, because God is faithful, because He will not allow you to be tempted beyond what you are able, because He offers a way out, flee.

What are we to flee from?

....

....

We often think of idols as graven images or ancient gods with temples and statues. Really, idols take all shapes and forms. We were made with worship in mind, created for God's glory, like we talked about in the first week. Because we were made for it, we are constantly worshiping something. Whatever we worship that is not God is an idol. It becomes an idol when we are willing to sin in order to gain access to it, or when we commit sins when we are deprived of it.

For example, say my favorite band is in town playing a show. I want to go to their show, but it's sold out. If I am willing to cheat or steal or lie in order to get tickets, the show has become my idol. Or if upon not getting tickets, I lash out in anger or gossip or become envious, the show has become my idol.

That example may be a little outlandish, but this happens in our lives more than we even realize. I have idolized myself most of my life. Before I realized this, I never would have said, "Oh, when I'm not worshiping God, I like to worship myself." But once I did realize I am my own biggest idol, more and more things made sense.

I care about how others think about me because I want them to serve the same god I do—myself. I worry because it gives me a sense of control, putting me in the place of God. Everything I do serves and worships someone. Fleeing from idolatry means we are constantly putting off the temptation to serve anyone or anything aside from the one true God.

The Ten Commandments begin:

Then God spoke all these words:

2   I am the Lord your God, who brought you out of the land of Egypt, out of the place of slavery.

3   Do not have other gods besides me.

4   Do not make an idol for yourself, whether in the shape of anything in the heavens above or on the earth below or in the waters under the earth. 5 Do not bow in worship to them, and do not serve them; for I, the Lord your God, am a jealous God, punishing the children for the fathers' iniquity, to the third and fourth generations of those who hate me, 6 but showing faithful love to a thousand generations of those who love me and keep my commands.

Exodus 20:1-3

In light of what we've learned, why do you think the Commandments begin this way?

....

....

What does it mean that God is a jealous God?

....

....

Our God is the only one worthy of worship. The one true God who made the heavens and the earth and everything in them deserves our undivided worship. He describes Himself as jealous because worship and service belong to Him. He lays His claim on our lives, our hearts, and our worship because they are His. He is jealous for what is His.

How does it make you feel to know that God is jealous for you?

....

....

Our God, the high priest who understands your temptations, who offers you a way out, does so because He loves you. He wants what is best for you and He is the best for you. Worship Him only, fleeing from the idols that easily entrap us.

The Bride Unblemished

I don't know if you're married or if you ever have been. I have never been married, but I've walked the aisle ahead of many of my friends and sat in witness as they vow to love their spouses for the rest of their lives. Despite the fact that I haven't had one myself, I love weddings.

All the lace and flowers and candles and dancing and hashtags—I'm here for all of it. Having been a bridesmaid and a friend of many more brides, I'm aware of all the work that goes into the day. Aside from the actual relationship, the bride and groom spend months planning every detail. They secure a location, they figure out a guest list, they send invites, and they decide on their wardrobe. Flowers are purchased and arranged with care. Food is prepared. The perfect playlist is curated.

Then there's the bride herself. The bride planned and tanned and everything in between, perhaps for her entire life, for this moment. She has imagined it a thousand times. Weddings typically last a few hours, but this bride worked for this moment.

Have you been a bride? If so, list a few of the things you did to prepare for the day of your wedding. If not, list a few things you've seen other brides do to prepare.

....

....

....

....

What is your favorite part of a wedding?

....

....

I'll tell you mine. It comes after the bridesmaids have walked down the aisle, the doors are closed, and the music changes. Perhaps it's a fancy church wedding and the doors are ornate and the music comes from an organ. Or perhaps it's in a field with the father of the bride blocking our view and the music plays from an iPod. The minister tells everyone to rise. We all stand and turn, and there is the bride.

A gasp echoes through the crowd. You can hear whispers of, "Oh!" and "Beautiful!" and "Can you see?" I cry every time. And half the time I can't even see her because I'm short and we're all standing.

READ EPHESIANS 5:22-33. Don't skim it—I know it's tempting if you aren't married, especially.

I used to skim this section, thinking it only somewhat applied to my unmarried self. But as I was reading this passage one day, verses 25-27 jumped out to me because they remind me of my favorite part of weddings. If we are believers in Jesus, we are part of the church. The church, as opposed to "a church," describes the group of believers as a whole. The church is global and timeless. We are all a part of the church.

Therefore, as believers, we are all His bride.

Notice who does the actions in verses 25-27. Who is it (circle one)?

1.   **Christ**

2.   **The Bride**

Jesus gave Himself for us so that we might be made holy. He cleansed us. He clothed us in splendor, without a spot, without a wrinkle, without a blemish. He made us holy.

Why did He do this?

....

Jesus Christ did this because He loves us and He wants us to be presented to Him without spot, without wrinkle, without a blemish—like a bride on her wedding day.

Can you imagine the day we are made whole again and presented to Jesus, our bridegroom? I imagine there will be a gasp in the room. We will be perfect because He is perfect and He made us perfect.

How does the fact that Jesus makes us perfect for Himself change your thoughts on submitting to Him?

....

....

....

....

Now let's look at verse 29 below:

For no one ever hates his own flesh but provides and cares for it, just as Christ does for the church.
Ephesians 5:29

Do you agree or disagree that no one ever hates their own flesh? Why or why not?

....

....

Yesterday we talked about the idol of self. Sometimes this idol doesn't make sense. It seems like if we don't like the way we look we don't worship ourselves or love ourselves, yet we love ourselves in the weirdest ways. For me, it looks like putting my preferences above everyone else's, being selfish and inwardly focused. I love myself by making an idol of myself and hoping others will join me in the illusion that the world revolves around me. Sometimes this means that I spend my money on myself before helping others, and sometimes this means that I lie awake at night worrying because it gives me a sense of control in my life. In the same way, we might deny ourselves the food we need or overindulge because of a desire to control.

Loving ourselves can look like confidence, but often it looks like a lack of confidence. We love ourselves and don't live up to our own high standards of perfection for our self-made gods. We don't hate our own flesh. We love it enough to provide for it and care for it, even if our provision and care doesn't work. We aren't God, after all. We may think we know what is best, what is care, what is provision, but He knows better.

READ ROMANS 8:28-29. What does it mean to be conformed?

....

....

I once had a teacher who said it like this: If I want to be conformed to the image of Miranda Kerr, for example, it won't be an easy process. With all the money in the world, the right surgeons, a killer workout routine, I might be able to eventually look like Miranda Kerr. But it will be painful, hard work. It will be costly. Looking like Miranda Kerr might be fun, but getting there would be the opposite.

You've probably heard verse 28 recited when something goes wrong. "All things work together for the good." People usually stop there, but Paul continues. God works everything together for the good of those who love Him, who are called according to His purpose. And what is His purpose? What is "the good"?

That we might be conformed to the image of His Son.

We are made in God's image, but we are not great little reflections most of the time. If we really want to represent God fully and well, we will have to be conformed to the image of Jesus. In other words, we will have to be "in splendor, without spot or wrinkle or anything like that, but holy and blameless" (Ephesians 5:27).

Think about some things in your life that would have to be reshaped, or perhaps cut out completely, in order for you to be conformed to the image of Jesus. Pray, asking God to help you have the courage and the humility to begin to reshape and conform to Him in those areas. Ask Him to help you put those things off and renew your mind. Ask Him to reveal to you through His Word what you should put on instead.

Jesus lived up to the standards so we don't have to. He made us His holy, unblemished bride. He knows how to provide and care for His body, the church. He loves us enough to conform us to His image, even when it's momentarily painful.

We just have
to submit to His
authority and care.

DAY 4

Reflection

What I learned about Jesus this week through Scripture:

....

....

....

....

What I learned about myself this week through His Word:

....

....

....

....

Things I need to ask God for help in putting off, renewing my mind, and putting on:

....

....

....

....

Alyssa asked this week that you start to ask God about the lies you are believing about yourself. Write out any He revealed to you:

....

....

....

....

....

....

....

....

Week 4

VIDEO TIME

REVIEW QUESTIONS:

1. Read Ephesians 5:1-19 together or in groups. Practice pointing out the things we are to "put off," and their opposites, what we are to "put on" instead.

2. Which fruit of the Spirit do you most easily exhibit? Which one is the biggest struggle for you? How can the group pray to help you with that one this week?

3. Have you ever felt you were alone in your struggles? What helped you to see you were not?

4. Does knowing Jesus is our high priest who understands our temptations give you hope? Why or why not?

5. What is your favorite part of a wedding?

6. How does knowing Christ works to make us holy help you to submit to Him?

WATCH THE VIDEO TEACHING SESSION.

VIDEO QUESTIONS:

1. How would your life be different if you felt victorious?

....

....

....

....

2. Read Ephesians 6:10-18 together. Which piece of armor do you have the most difficulty putting on?

....

....

....

....

3. What does it look like in your everyday life to stand firm?

....

....

....

4. How does it change your thoughts and feelings toward your body when you know you are God's
    temple?

....

....

....

....

5. Which aspect of what Alyssa said is the most difficult for you—calling out a lie or covering it with
    truth?

....

....

....

....

6. Pray together that God will show you who He is and who He says you are this week.

This week's Next Right Step from our friends at FINDING*balance*®:

Write down one part of your body - ***or something your body allows you to do*** - that you're thankful for.

DAY 1

Think on These Things

When I was younger, I had a tshirt that said, "Whatever!" on the front, and on the back had Philippians 4:8 written out. My friend's dad challenged me to memorize it since I wore it on my back, so I did.

Obviously, I was a super cool kid with a refined fashion sense, but I didn't realize my favorite shirt would contained the key for life transformation until years later.

Let's review the three-step process for change:

1. **Put** _____

2. _____ **your mind**

3. **Put** _____

We've talked about steps 1 and 3, but today we're going to camp out on step two. Step two is perhaps the most difficult simply because it's kind of vague. I can easily see how to put off lying and put on truth telling, but renewing my mind? How does that even work?

Take a stab at it. How does renewing your mind work?

....

....

Whenever I think of renewing, I generally think of renewing a subscription to a magazine or a streaming service. The Greek word used for renew in Ephesians 4:23 can also mean to renovate or be spiritually transformed. A renovation helps me understand the process a little better.

A good before and after photo will stop me in my Instagram scrolling. I like to see transformations and renovations, especially if the after looks a lot different from the before. Sometimes, they're not even comparable—Was there a wall there before?

Renovations generally cause more upheaval than a simple coat of paint. Walls will be moved, appliances bought, floors torn up. But the end results bring gasps and reveals worthy of reality TV.

Our goal: renovate our minds. Gut them out, rebuild, make them beautiful. Philippians 4:8 will help us do that, but first let's look at 2 Corinthians 10:5.

READ 2 CORINTHIANS 10:2-5. What does it look like to wage war *according to the flesh*?

....

....

In these verses, the term *flesh* represents our physical selves. We live here on earth and do battle against many things, both physical and spiritual, on a daily basis. We battle against our own sinful desires. We battle against our bodies. We battle against our hearts and thoughts.

However, we aren't bringing weapons of the flesh to fight this battle. We bring weapons God has empowered to demolish strongholds. Through Him, we can tear down the walls of our minds. Get your hard hat on; here we go!

What are the two action words in verses 4-5?

....

....

Demolish. Take captive. Our arguments and proud things are not going down without a fight. It's like any renovation project—it takes up far more time and effort than you ever imagined or planned it would.

We aren't using our own weapons for this, though, remember. We are using weapons God has empowered.

Turn to Ephesians 6:10-18 and list out the weapons God equips us with.

....

....

What is our struggle against (v. 12)?

....

....

We're not struggling against flesh and blood. We're struggling against the powers of darkness. I don't know about you, but I for one am glad I'm not given my own weapons to use in this fight.

We do battle against our sin with truth, righteousness, the gospel of peace, faith, salvation, and the Word of God. The seventh weapon in this armory? Prayer (v. 18).

So, how do we actually start this renovation of our minds? How do we really start taking thoughts captive? This is where "Whatever!" comes in.

Turn to Philippians 4:8. Circle the things below we are to think about:

whatever is true	whatever we feel	whatever others are talking about
whatever we want	whatever is honorable	whatever we hear on TV
whatever is just	whatever is pure	whatever is fun
whatever is newsworthy	whatever is lovely	whatever is commendable

Okay, so some of those are pretty obvious, but we often let our minds dwell on everything but the list Paul gives us. That's why we have to get our weapons ready. We are to take all those other thoughts captive, hold them prisoner, and replace them with these things.

Have you ever tried to think of nothing? It's impossible. Even when we meditate on God's Word, and try to focus on him alone, it's hard to keep other thoughts from creeping in. We can't just put off false thoughts or just take them captive. We have to put on other thoughts. We have to replace them in our brains. If we're not careful, we replace them with things that are just as bad. To continue the illustration I used earlier, we replace mud with muddy water.

How do you think we begin to replace our false thoughts with things that are morally excellent and praiseworthy?

....

....

It is not an easy or fun process, but believe me when I say it is worth the effort. Once we learn to replace our thoughts, we know the formula for change. What we think changes the way we feel which changes the way we act. Renovating our minds kick starts the whole process.

If we're going to replace our thoughts, we have to have something to replace them with. We can find things that are true, honorable, lovely, pure, just, and commendable in God's Word.

Let's practice together. Grab a concordance or go to a website or app with a Bible you can use to search for specific words or topics (BibleGateway.com is one). Look up each of the following words and jot down a verse or two that speaks to those concepts. I've added one to each word just to get you started.

True - *Psalm 119:160*

Honorable - *Luke 6:45*

Just - *Isaiah 30:18*

Pure - *Psalm 18:30*

Lovely - *Psalm 147:1*

Commendable (or admirable) - *2 Corinthians 10:18*

Excellent - *Psalm 8:1*

Praiseworthy - *Isaiah 63:7*

We're going to work on memorizing Scripture the rest of this week and next. By memorizing Scripture, by praying it back to God, we are dwelling on it. We are dwelling on things that are true, honorable, just, pure, lovely, commendable, excellent, and praiseworthy. When we dwell on these things, the falsehoods and lies and other gods are pushed aside. There isn't room for what we've already put off and we've decided to tear down that wall, anyway.

To close today, choose one of the verses above and write it out as a prayer to God. Thank Him for showing us what to dwell on, thank Him for being One who is true, honorable, just, pure, lovely, commendable, excellent, and praiseworthy, and ask for His help in renewing your mind. He would love to do just that!

I (Don't) Got This

After learning important words like mama, dada, no, and mine, toddlers typically move onto something like myself. Everything is "Do it myself." They buckle their own car seats, brush their own teeth, pick out their own clothes. Try to help a toddler doing things by herself, and you'll be met with screams, dozens of "No no no no!"s, and possibly a full-fledged tantrum. We want children to learn independence and skills necessary for life, but toddlers are usually pretty bad at doing things.

I stood in a cold parking garage, already running late, for about five minutes one day waiting on a friend's two year old to buckle her car seat strap, a task that would have literally taken me seconds to do. (Before you judge my parenting and which battles I choose to fight, please know that I was just the babysitter. My goal was simply not to bring back a child with tear-streaks on her face.)

We look at these toddler struggles and have to laugh because, well, toddlers are just cute. We also laugh because we know we could do the task so much better, but we also understand the need to do things "myself." We all want to be in control and independent.

In what areas of your life do you feel you have the most control? The least?

....

....

How do you see yourself trying to control the circumstances of your life? How successful are you?

....

....

Most of the time, we cannot control the circumstances of our lives. The actions of those around us, the culture we live in, nature as a whole, we can't control. Many times, because we are sinners and idol-makers, we attempt to control the things we can't by wrongly controlling those we can.

If we can't control the actions of our parents, the words of our friends (or enemies), the expectations of our teachers, we sometimes turn to the things we feel like we can control—the way we look, the food we eat, how much we exercise.

We tell ourselves the lie, "I need control."

Have you ever felt this way? Explain.

....

....

....

Do you agree that "I need control" is a lie? Why or why not?

....

....

Look at some biblical examples of people who tried to take control of their circumstances and write the outcome of their takeover in the chart.

Person	Scripture	Consequences
Peter	John 18:7-11	
Rebekah	Genesis 27:5-46	
Ananias and Sapphira	Acts 5:1-11	
David	2 Samuel 11:1-15,26-27	

When we attempt to control our lives by the way we eat, we end up allowing food to control us. It may take a while, but we will get to the point to being controlled by the revulsion of food, by the compulsion to remain in control, and by the chains of addiction we'll bear.

Needing to control is a lie because we can only learn to control our reactions to the situations in our lives, and even then, we need Jesus to help us. Self-control is a fruit of the Spirit, so He helps us to control ourselves. Only God is truly in control.

Read the following verses and jot down what God controls in each one:

Proverbs 16:9

....

....

Isaiah 45:6-7

....

....

Matthew 6:26-32

....

....

Most of the time control and manipulation of our bodies as a means to control come from a place of fear and anxiety. We want to control because we are afraid of what might happen if we are not in control.

If God is in control of all things, and we are afraid of what might happen if we are not in control, what does that say about how we trust God's control?

....

....

....

When we try to take over our circumstances, we are trying to replace God with ourselves. We're telling ourselves the lie, "I need to control this." We don't need to because of who God is—sovereign over everything in our lives.

Remember the three-step process to change? Put off the old, renew our minds, put on the new. We need to first put off the lie that we need to be in control. Then we need to dwell on what is true.

Look up the following verses and select one that speaks to you especially today.

Psalm 56:3

Isaiah 41:10

John 14:27

Philippians 4:4-7

1 Peter 5:7

Write the verse you selected on an index card or a sticky note and put it in a place you'll see it when you are most tempted to think, "I need to be in control." Maybe that's your mirror, your refrigerator, your bedside table, or your dashboard. You may even make multiple copies!

If you are continually telling yourself the lie of needing to control, memorize the verse you wrote down. This is your mind renovation tool. Whenever you start the thought, "I need to control this," recite the verse.

You won't want to do it at first. It will be difficult to turn the wheels of your mind toward the Bible. But the more you do it, the easier it will get. And if you're thinking about God's sovereignty and His promises, you won't be able to think about controlling your situation.

And if you're thinking about God's sovereignty and His promises, you won't be able to think about controlling your situation.

DAY 3

Appearances

The problem of appearances is nothing new. We've had a weird relationship with our physical bodies since Genesis 3. However, social media brings incorrect standards for our looks to our attention constantly. We carry around little fashion magazines and critics in our pockets wherever we go.

Standards for beauty change like fashion. Depending on your era, your location, and your culture, your ideal body type might be completely different from mine. But we all struggle to try to meet those standards. When we don't meet those standards we begin to tell ourselves lies.

"I'm not beautiful."

"I need to be a certain size."

"I should look more like her."

In Matthew 23, we read of people who were very concerned with keeping up appearances.

Turn to Matthew 23 in your Bible and read verses 5 and 25-28.

Phylacteries and tassels were religious items worn by the Pharisees at the time of Jesus.

What is the Pharisees' motivation in verse 5?

....

....

When we strive to look a certain way, we are also misplacing our motivation. They made themselves an idol—look at me! If we are obsessed with our appearances, we are misplacing our motivations.

READ 2 CORINTHIANS 5:9. What should our motivation be?

....

....

How do we please God? Read Matthew 17:5 and Mark 1:11 for a hint.

....

....

Jesus pleased God. He lived a life without sin and gave glory to His Father. If we want to please God, we should be imitators of Christ (Ephesians 5:1). We take on the righteousness of Christ when we believe and follow Him.

Look back to Matthew 23:25-28. What are the two comparisons Jesus makes to the Pharisees and scribes in these verses?

....

....

Have you seen this in your own life—an outward appearance that does not match your inward self? How so?

....

....

The Pharisees were hypocrites because they kept all the rules and then some. They looked very religious with their phylacteries and long tassels and laws. They appeared religious but God sees the heart. He knew they were full of greed. He knew they were full of lawlessness on the inside.

When our motivations are mixed up, we begin to think we need to look put together on the outside more than we need to be at peace on the inside. We end up striving to follow rules of the way we look, what we wear, how we exercise, what foods we eat and don't eat, instead of living in the grace of God.

READ EPHESIANS 2:1-5 BELOW. Underline all the phrases and words that talk about our old selves, before Christ.

And you were dead in your trespasses and sins 2 in which you previously lived according to the ways of this world, according to the ruler of the power of the air, the spirit now working in the disobedient. 3 We too all previously lived among them in our fleshly desires, carrying out the inclinations of our flesh and thoughts, and we were by nature children under wrath as the others were also. 4 But God, who is rich in mercy, because of his great love that he had for us, 5 made us alive with Christ even though we were dead in trespasses. You are saved by grace!

How would you define grace?

....

....

Because God loves us so much, even when we were dead, He made us alive with Christ. We were given what we didn't deserve—salvation and life with Him. That is grace.

When we live knowing we are loved that much, knowing that grace covers our sins and weaknesses, we will not be as concerned with looking a certain way. We will break free from the lies that cause us so much harm.

We'll put off the lies of appearances and put on the truth of love and grace and who we are in Christ.

Read the following verses and select one to write down to place in every spot you're tempted to think, "I don't look the way I should."

Genesis 1:31

Psalm 139:14

Luke 12:27-28

Ephesians 2:8-9

1 Peter 1:3-4

If the soundtrack in your mind continually tells you to look a certain way or keep up with appearances, take one of these verses and memorize it this week. Work to replace the thoughts of looks with thoughts of His grace, mercy, and love. Hard work will pay off, and eventually the soundtrack will begin to change.

DAY 4

What have you learned from the Scriptures about who God is?

....

....

....

What did you learn from the Scriptures about what God says about you?

....

....

....

What thoughts are you working to remove from your mind? What Scriptures has God shown you to replace them with?

....

....

....

Praise God for the truth of His Word. Confess to God the times you've told yourself lies.

Ask forgiveness and for help renovating your mind this week.

Week 5

VIDEO TIME

REVIEW QUESTIONS:

1. Share a few of the verses you found that express things that are true, just, pure, excellent, praiseworthy, honorable, and commendable.

....

....

2. Does it comfort you to know God has given us weapons to renew our minds? Why or why not?

....

....

3. Which of the verses about control spoke to you the most? Share a little about that.

....

....

4. Which of the verses about God's grace and love spoke to you the most? Share about it in the group.

....

....

5. What stuck out to you anew from this week's study?

....

....

WATCH THE VIDEO TEACHING FOR WEEK 5.

VIDEO QUESTIONS:

1. Do you have a mentor? Share a bit about her.

....

....

....

This week's Next Right Step from our friends at FINDING*balance*®:

If you have a mentor in your life, reach out to them this week and share what you've been learning. If you don't have a mentor, ask God to lead you to someone who could be that in your life.

2. Read 1 Corinthians 13 together as a group. Have you lived with a misunderstanding of love? In what ways?

....

....

....

3. How does knowing who God is and His characteristics change how you think about yourself?

....

....

....

DAY 1

My Pleasure

Advertising agencies know our deepest desires. They know when they're trying to sell a product, if they can make it seem comfortable or pleasurable, we're all in. We'll buy a mattress that claims to provide a comfortable place to sleep. We buy certain foods because they are said to taste better. We buy cleaning supplies that make our lives easier and more pleasant. We purchase cars with heated seats.

We seek comfort.

For a lot of us, food provides comfort and pleasure. God made food to keep us alive, yes, but He also created it to be pleasant. He lends His creativity to chefs and bakers to create delicious concoctions. He tells us to taste and see that He is good (Psalm 34:8).

The problem comes when we turn to food to provide comfort, instead of turning to God.

We often tell ourselves the lie, "If I eat (or don't eat), my pain will go away."

We make little gods out of our food, expecting it to heal our discomfort, make us happy, or help us to be better people. When something goes wrong in our lives, instead of turning to the truth of God's Word, we gorge ourselves on chocolate or potato chips. When we feel alone and hurt, we think a cup of coffee will give us a better attitude. Or maybe we do the opposite, ridding our pantries and refrigerators of everything because we believe getting rid of access food will also rid our lives of pain.

Have you ever turned to food to make you feel better? What was the result?

....

....

READ 2 CORINTHIANS 1:3-7. What do these verses tell us about suffering?

....

....

Suffering is inevitable. We suffer because a long time ago, the first man and the first woman disobeyed God and we continue in their footsteps. Our world is broken and while we wait for Jesus to come and make it whole again, affliction haunts us.

What do these verses tell you about God?

....

....

Our God is "the God of all comfort." He comforts us. We don't have to turn to food or any other thing to bring us peace from our hardships.

READ MATTHEW 11:28-30. Who does Jesus ask to come to Him?

....

....

Jesus was speaking here in contrast to the heavy yoke of those like the Pharisees and scribes who put laws on top of laws. The people easily wearied trying to keep up with laws in order to be religious. Jesus asks them to trade those rules and regulations for His easy yoke of rest.

He promises the same to us. When we are burdened from the world or from trying to be good and religious, Jesus stands, ready to trade yokes. He offers healing and comfort. We don't have to turn to food, which will only provide a temporary pleasure, to be comforted. We have the One who can provide real comfort and real rest!

READ 1 TIMOTHY 4:1-5. For what purpose did God create food?

....

Verse 4 says that everything created by God is good. How are we to receive food?

....

Food sustains us. Food also evokes in us gratitude and thanksgiving to the One who provides it for us. Food, like all of creation, should glorify God, not become a god in our lives. When we turn to food to comfort, heal, or provide the pleasure only God can truly provide us, we are robbing Him of the praise and glory He deserves.

Today, instead of listing several verses to put on instead of the lie of "Food will take away my pain," we are going to put on the prayer of thanksgiving and longing for God alone.

Now read Psalm 63:1-8 below. Personalize the words of David making them your own prayer. If a verse stands out to you, write it down and place it on your refrigerator door or pantry to remind you to give thanks to God for food and to seek Him rather than food when you need comfort.

1
God, you are my God; I eagerly seek you.
I thirst for you;
my body faints for you
in a land that is dry, desolate, and without water.

2
So I gaze on you in the sanctuary
to see your strength and your glory.

3
My lips will glorify you
because your faithful love is better than life.

4
So I will bless you as long as I live;
at your name, I will lift up my hands.

5
You satisfy me as with rich food;
my mouth will praise you with joyful lips.

6
When I think of you as I lie on my bed,
I meditate on you during the night watches

7
because you are my helper;
I will rejoice in the shadow of your wings.

8
I follow close to you;
your right hand holds on to me.

DAY 2

Perfect

As I write this, the Olympics are on TV. We watch each night as athletes who've trained their whole lives work for a perfect score. And anything can throw them off perfection—a chip of ice, a loose knot, sleeping in a different bed the night before. Perfect scores are nearly impossible to obtain, which is why we give gold medals to those who come close.

They work their whole lives and in 1/100th of a second, perfect can be ruined.

Would you consider yourself a perfectionist? Why or why not?

....

....

I never considered myself a perfectionist. For the most part, I'm okay with not being perfect. But I have always wanted to be as close to perfect as I could be. If I wasn't going to get a 100 on a test, I asked for extra credit. As soon as I realized I wasn't a talented singer, I quit the choir. If I had a daily Bible reading plan and missed a day, I started over completely.

When we tell ourselves that we can be perfect, we are telling ourselves a lie.

We can't.

READ ROMANS 5:12. How did sin enter the world?

....

....

Is anyone exempt from being a sinner?

....

....

Sin entered the world in Genesis 3. In paradise, Adam and Eve sinned, and we humans continue to sin. Even the closest to perfect among us has disobeyed God.

But there is hope.

READ ROMANS 5:8-11. When did Jesus die for us?

....

....

We don't have to be perfect for Jesus to die for our sins and cover us with His sacrifice.

What is proven through God sending His Son for us (v. 8)?

....

....

What does Jesus' sacrifice mean for our sins?

....

....

We've already been over this, but we can never go over the good news of Jesus too many times! Jesus' sacrifice made it so that we can be righteous through Him. That is the best news of all time!

We can't be perfect, but we can be seen as perfect by God through His Son.

How does knowing that Jesus was the perfect sacrifice for your sins help you to put away the need for perfection?

....

....

Another way we put away perfection is to put on contentment. For those of us who feel like we need everything—including, but not limited to, ourselves—to be perfect, one of the hardest things can be to find contentment in the inevitable imperfections of life.

We always think, if _____ were _____, everything would be perfect.

Maybe you fill in those blanks in one of these ways:

If I were skinnier, everything would be perfect.
If I worked out more, everything would be perfect.
If I could get his attention, everything would be perfect.
If I didn't eat so much, everything would be perfect.
If I looked like her, everything would be perfect.

How would you fill in those blanks?

If _____ , everything would be perfect.

READ PHILIPPIANS 4:11-13. What had Paul learned to do?

....

....

Paul, the man who wrote this letter, was formerly a bit of a perfectionist. He had been a religious leader, at the top of an Ivy-League-equivalent class. He persecuted Christians before he came to know Jesus. Once he became a Christian, he was beaten, thrown in prison, stoned, and scorned. Yet he learned to be content in every situation.

Do you know someone who seems to be content in every situation? What is he or she like?

....

....

What would it look like for you to be content?

....

....

We find a lot of freedom in contentment. Freedom to be ourselves. Freedom to let go of insecurities and striving. Freedom to rest in the grace of God. Maybe this sounds impossible for you right now, but remember verse 13 says that all things are possible with God. You can be content. You can be free.

Read the following verses and select one to write down to place in every spot you're tempted to think, "I need to be perfect."

2 Chronicles 20:17

Psalm 18:32

Matthew 6:33

Ephesians 2:8-10

1 Peter 3:3-4

Pray to close out today, thanking God for making you perfect in Jesus. Ask for His help in overcoming the lie that you need to be perfect on your own.

Thank Him
for making all
things possible.

DAY 3

Please Like Me

We all want to be liked. Social media platforms know this. They've created a whole system based on you getting other people to like you and what you're doing. We crave those little hearts and thumbs ups and smiley faces.

But this problem existed before social media, too. We "dress to impress" and just want people to say we're pretty or funny or they love our shoes. We are constantly craving attention and approval from everyone we meet.

We tell ourselves the lie, "If I'm _____ , everyone will like me."

What have you put in that blank?

If I'm _____ , everyone will like me.

A few years ago, a friend of mine implied that I wasn't "cool." She didn't really mean it as a dig. At the time, I was a grown up. I wasn't in high school or junior high. But I thought about not being cool for weeks. It hurt my feelings. I reevaluated all the clothes I'd been wearing, what I'd been listening to, what shows I had watched. I wanted so badly to change something so that I would be seen as cool.

People-pleasing sneaks up on you like that.

There's nothing wrong with wanting to be winsome and with wanting others to like you. It becomes a problem when we hold the opinion of humans higher than God's opinion or when we choose to disobey God in order to get or keep the approval of humans.

Lots of people in the Bible sought the approval of humans over God, but today we're going to look at a time when Moses almost missed out on God's plan for his life because of his desire for approval.

READ EXODUS 4:1-17. What was Moses afraid of?

....

Have you ever been there—afraid to do something you felt God was telling you to do because you were afraid of what others might think? Explain.

....

....

....

....

If you're familiar with the story of Moses or the story of the Bible as a whole, you know that Moses ended up being one of the greatest leaders in history. He led God's people out of Egypt and through the desert. He carried down God's Law to the people and instructed them on how to live. He wrote several books of the Bible, detailing the history of the world and God's people.

Rewrite verse 11 in your own words.

....

....

God created us. He created you the way you are on purpose. He created you for His glory, remember (Isaiah 43:7)? If we're created for His glory, then we need to spend our time trying to please Him, not other image-bearers.

How do we do please God?

....

....

READ ROMANS 12. What is our true worship, according to verse 1?

....

This chapter tells us how to present ourselves as a living sacrifice and how to live as those who are pleasing God instead of humans. It tells us how to behave as those who believe.

When we do these things, we will no longer be conformed to this age—to the things others want from us. We will be transformed and we will be able to discern the will of God. When we do all of these things, it will be a sacrifice. These things are not easy to do.

Look at verses 3-8. What do these tell us about other people?

....

....

We all have different gifts. God made us that way. He made us with different giftings that we are to use for His glory. Part of being in His body means that we support and cheer on one another in our various giftings. We aren't envious of others because we are keeping our hearts and heads focused on using our giftings for His glory. We'll cheer on one another to do the same.

Make a list of all the qualities we are to "put on," or things we should do, in verses 9-21:

....

....

....

....

Which of those things are easiest for you? Which are the most challenging?

....

....

When we are rejoicing with those who rejoice and living at peace with everyone, we won't have time to think, "If only I were _____, everyone would like me." We'll quit striving for attention and learn to point it to the One who is worthy of all worship and praise and honor.

Read the following verses and select one to write down to place in every spot you're tempted to think, "If _____ , everyone would like me."

1 Samuel 16:7

Proverbs 29:25

1 Corinthians 1:27-29

Galatians 1:10

Colossians 3:23

1 Thessalonians 2:4

Pray as you close out today, asking God to help you desire to please Him above others.

Thank Him for
loving you and
for creating you
for His glory.

DAY 4

What did God teach you about Himself through Scripture this week?

....

....

....

What did He teach you about yourself?

....

....

....

How can you apply His Word to your life this week?

....

....

....

Journal the answers to the questions Alyssa asked in the video:

....

....

....

....

God, can you show me when this started?

....

....

....

....

Why did my younger self feel the need to do this?

....

....

....

....

Pray, asking God to help your views of Him align with Scripture.

Week 6

VIDEO TIME

REVIEW QUESTIONS:

1. Which verses from this week's study stood out to you?

....

2. What lies do you tend to return to time and again?

....

3. How can we be praying for you this week?

....

WATCH THE VIDEO TEACHING SESSION FOR SESSION 6.

VIDEO DISCUSSION:

1. How have you been isolated in your struggle in the past?

....

2. Who are people in your life who point you to the truth? If you don't have such a person, who can you talk to about doing that for you in the future?

....

This week's Next Right Step from our friends at FINDING*balance*®:

Identify one thought you will work on changing for the next 63 days.

DAY 1

We Need Each Other

I f you take a piece of string and double it up, it's stronger. If you take a piece of string and triple it—maybe even braid it—it's even stronger. One time my friends and I tested this theory with some old leather shoelaces. We would stretch them out and easily break through only one (it was old leather, weathered and brittle). When we doubled it up, we could still snap it in half, though it took a little more time. But once we braided it, we couldn't break it.

Now this experiment would vary depending on the type of string or cord you're using, but the point is that three are stronger than one.

READ ECCLESIASTES 4:9-12. How would you sum up these verses?

....

....

When we are together, we are stronger. The road you are walking to freedom is not an easy one. There will be cold nights and trips and falls and temptations seemingly trying to break you. That's why we need each other. As Alyssa and Sadie said in the video, we tend to go into isolation when we are fighting against sin. We tend to want to be alone, not believing others, not sharing our struggles.

The truth is, we need someone to help us up when we fall—when we fall to temptation again. We need someone who will be with us in the nights of our faith when we need someone else to speak the truth to us because we have forgotten. We need a community of people who will band together to fight the lies with the truth.

Do you have people like this in your life? If so, tell about them. If not, take a moment to pray God will bring you godly friends to be this community for you.

....

....

....

Not to be overly dramatic, but we've entered into a battlefield. We're bringing truth against lies, hope against despair, grace against shame. We have God's armor to fight with (Ephesians 6:10-18), but we're going to need fellow soldiers. We're going to need those who will fight with us and those who have already won battles in their own lives.

One of my favorite stories in Scripture is in Exodus 17.

READ EXODUS 17:8-13. What was the problem in these verses?

....

....

What was the solution?

....

....

When Moses raised his arms, Joshua prevailed. But like all of us, Moses grew weary. He needed the support of his friends. They couldn't hold their own arms up in place of his. They couldn't do the work for him. Instead, they had to come along and support him in his work. They held up his arms for the rest of the battle.

Sometimes we will get tired of repeating the truth to ourselves. We'll get tired of putting off and putting on. We may even try to just go to sleep in our muddy clothes, thinking we'll clean up in the morning. It will seem like a lot of work sometimes, because it is.

That's when we need community. We need those around us who will hold up our arms during the fight. No one else can renew your mind for you. No one else can put off the lies and replace them with the truth in your mind. But they can support you. They can remind you of the truth you need to hear. They can pray for you.

The scariest part may be letting them know you're doing battle and your arms are getting tired.

What's holding you back from enlisting a group of friends to help you battle the lies?

....

How can you battle the lie you just listed with truth? Break out a concordance and find some verses that speak to the truth of community, love, grace, and hope.

....

....

We need people in our lives who will feed us Scripture when we can't discern the truth from the lies ourselves. We need friends who will ask us, "What is true, what is pure, what is lovely?" We need people walking with us who continually point us to Jesus and to the hope we have in Him.

We not only need people like that who will walk beside us, but also those who are ahead of us on the path to freedom. We need mentors who will help us discern the truth and walk in it.

Paul was such a mentor to Timothy. He called Timothy his son in the faith and told him, "What you have heard from me in the presence of many witnesses, commit to faithful men who will be able to teach others also" (2 Timothy 2:2). He not only taught Timothy the truth, but modeled it.

Do you have someone in your life you'd consider a mentor? Tell about that person.

....

....

If not, pray that God will bring someone to mind. Make a plan to ask her to grab coffee.

We need each other's help in our journeys toward freedom. Once we know how to put off our sinful behaviors and the lies we tell ourselves, renew our minds, and put on things that will glorify Him, we will need accountability to stick to it. Thankfully, we have each other.

DAY 2

How May I Serve You?

More and more companies are looking to improve their customer service experiences. They work to give their employees the authority to make things right with a customer, no matter the expense. You've probably heard the stories—a shoe company overnighting special shoes for a wedding, a restaurant opening their doors to those stranded in an ice storm, a coffee shop saying, "This one's on us." Famously, when a customer says thank you at Chick-fil-A®, the employees reply, "My pleasure."

How does it make you feel when you encounter excellent customer service?

....

....

Along with putting on the truth, we are also to put on habits and behaviors that are opposite of the lies and sinful behaviors we took off. The same pattern that holds true for our thoughts—swapping out one for another—also holds true for our actions.

What do you think is the opposite of your temptation with food and/or body image?

....

....

READ GALATIANS 5:13-15. What should we use our freedom for?

....

....

Many times people will see the golden rule, or the call for us to love our neighbors as ourselves, as a mandate to love ourselves first. However, as we looked at previously, we already love ourselves. That's a given.

When we find true freedom from sin, from food, from lies, we are to use that freedom as an opportunity to serve others.

READ THE REST OF GALATIANS 5. Make a list of the things we are to put off and those we are to put on.

Put off:	Put on:

We made a list earlier in our study of the fruits of the Spirit. Those are the things we are to put on instead of the lies we believe.

Which of the fruits of the spirit do you think are the most opposite to your temptations?

....

....

What are some practical ways to put those on this week?

....

....

....

Verse 24 says, "Now those who belong to Christ Jesus have crucified the flesh with its passions and desires." Paul is talking about the renovations we did to our mind. In that way, we are crucifying our old ways, the things we put off. He's not painting a pretty picture, is he? It takes work to put off our old desires and our old lies and temptations. But if we belong to Jesus, we have the Holy Spirit to help us produce His fruit—love, joy, peace, patience, kindness, goodness, faithfulness, gentleness, and self control.

Turn to Philippians 2 and read verses 1-4. Write verse 4 below.

....

....

....

....

Who do you know who does a good job of this—putting others' interests above his or her own? Tell about a time when you saw that demonstrated.

....

....

....

....

Brainstorm a few people with whom you interact on a daily basis. They might be your family members, your friends, your neighbors, or even the barista at your local coffee shop. Make a list of a few of them in the left column of the chart below. In the right column, brainstorm some specific ways you can practically put their interests above your own this week.

Person	Way to put their interests above yours

The possibilities for considering someone else as more important than yourself are endless. Perhaps you offer to do a chore for someone or write them a note. Maybe you watch the kids so they can do something fun. Or maybe it's as simple as being with them when you'd rather be somewhere else.

When we think more about other people, other bearers of God's image, than we do ourselves, our minds are busy. Instead of worrying or trying to control or manipulate or striving for perfection, we'll be focused on serving and giving God glory. We will trade one for the other, putting on love and kindness and gentleness instead of self-focus.

Today spend some time writing notes or doing acts of service for other people. Send a text or an email to tell them you're thinking about them. Offer practical ways to help.

Pray for eyes to see opportunities to love others, to be unified in Christ, and to think of others more highly.

DAY 3

Thank You

When we're little, we often learn the "magic words"—please and thank you. We learn to say please to get what we want and we learn that we better follow it up with "thank you" if we want to remain in good graces. We learn to express gratitude even if we don't always feel it.

In the U.S., we even have an entire holiday based on gratitude. We give thanks for our friends and family and food. We express gratitude for the Lord's provision, in remembrance of how He provided centuries ago and in honor of how He continues to provide.

Whether you celebrate Thanksgiving as an official holiday or whatever your thoughts on it are, we can all use a reminder and a day off devoted to celebrating in gratitude. Gratitude is on the path of recovery from self-focus. When we spend time counting our blessings, we have less time to devote to worrying, seeking control, comparing, or striving for what's not real.

List five things you're thankful for right now. (Don't think too hard or long about this—just list the first five things you think of!)

1.
....

2.
....

3.
....

4.
....

5.
....

On a scale of 1 to 10, with 1 being "super easy" and 10 being "it took me forever," how easy was it for you to think of five things you're thankful for? (Circle your answer)

1   2   3   4   5   6   7   8   9   10

If we're all honest, we know that sometimes we can list a thousand things we're thankful for without even thinking, but other times it's difficult to even think of one thing. Sometimes we fill journals with praise and thanksgiving to God. Other times, we have to force out a thank you for even the seemingly simple things.

Read 1 Thessalonians 5:16-18 below.

Rejoice always, pray constantly, give thanks in everything; for this is God's will for you in Christ Jesus.

When does it say to rejoice?

....

How often should we pray?

....

....

In what circumstances should we give thanks?

....

....

When we're frustrated, when we're sad, when we're lonely, when we're angry, when we're celebrating, when we're grateful—in all the whens—we rejoice. We pray constantly, like breath, communing with our Provider. In good times, in bad times, in weird times, we give thanks. Rejoicing, praying, and giving thanks aren't presented as optional activities. We're commanded to do them. Even if we don't feel like it.

Do you know someone who has shown courage by giving thanks and rejoicing even in the midst of hardship? Tell how you saw them live that out.

....

....

....

....

When we replace the lies we tell ourselves with the freedom of thanksgiving, we begin to reshape our thoughts. A good place to begin is at the table.

In the chart below, note what happens each time food is served.

Scripture	Who is speaking?	What did they do before serving the food?
Matthew 14:19		
Mark 8:6-7		
Luke 22:19		
John 6:11,23		
Acts 27:33-36		

What can we learn from these biblical examples?

....

....

To find freedom from food, we must learn to give thanks. This will take practice and you probably won't feel grateful at first—maybe not even for a long time. Persevere! Eventually, our hearts and emotions will begin to follow the mind. We'll start to mean it when we say those magic words: "Thank you."

To end today, turn to Psalm 100 and read it as a prayer to God.

DAY 4

Spend today giving thanks to God for providing us with friends and mentors to cheer us on and hold us accountable. If you do not have such a community in your life, pray that He might bring you one.

Ask for opportunities and eyes to see ways to lift up others, putting their interests above your own.

Finally, start a list. Write down all the things you're thankful for today. Keep the list somewhere you can see it and add to it as much as possible.

Week 7

VIDEO TIME

REVIEW QUESTIONS:

1. Share about your community. Brag on your friends and mentors, telling how they work to cheer you on, to hold you accountable, and to point you to the truth.

....

....

....

....

2. Tell about an excellent customer service experience you've had.

....

....

....

3. Read Philippians 2:1-4 as a group. Share some of the ways you came up with to love others this week.

....

....

....

4. Select a few of the things you're thankful for to read to the group.

....

....

....

....

5. Ask how you can help put one another first, how you can encourage and serve one another this week.

....

....

WATCH THE VIDEO TEACHING FOR WEEK 7.

VIDEO DISCUSSION QUESTIONS:

1. What are some very practical steps you've taken in gaining a healthier relationship with food and exercise?

....

....

....

....

2.   Is there anything in your life that you used to hate, but now love, like Sadie was talking about?

....

....

3.   How can we encourage one another in the practical habits of health?

....

....

....

....

This week's Next Right Step from our friends at FINDING*balance*®:

Consider what area you need the most help in and choose one thing you will do next. This may be finding a nutritionist, choosing someone to be accountable to, or something else. If you need help finding resources, be sure to visit our friends at www.findingbalance.com/freedom

---
DAY 1

Freedom

Whenever I hear the word freedom spoken aloud, I want to yell it. FREEDOM!! Just me? Something about the word and the definition make me want to yell it out, maybe while running or pole vaulting. Isn't that a picture of freedom, too? Freedom to celebrate, to run, to yell, to leap!

When I think about the opposite of freedom, I think chains and entrapment and silence. Throughout this study, I hope and pray you have found freedom. I hope you've loosened the chains a bit and maybe raised your voice just a little.

READ HEBREWS 12:1-2. What are we supposed to do with every hindrance and sin that entangles us?

Before these verses, the writer of Hebrews talks about the faithful ones who came before us. Because these are our people—these are the witnesses who surround us speaking truth—we throw off any sin that entangles us. We cast aside everything that slows us down and keeps us from running full speed ahead toward Jesus. We could even yell "FREEDOM!" as we run (just a suggestion).

I pray that in this study you have learned to cast aside the hindrances and the sin as we put them off. I pray that your mind is being renewed and you're putting on your running shoes.

Who do we keep our eyes on in this race?

When we keep our eyes on Jesus, we keep them off ourselves. We live for His glory and our good. When our eyes are on Jesus, we are automatically dwelling on what is true, honorable, just, pure, lovely, commendable, excellent, and praiseworthy because He is all of those things.

Practically, what does it look like in your life to keep your eyes on Christ?

We keep our eyes on Jesus by reading His Word, being among His people, and staying in daily communion with Him through prayer. We serve in His name, we worship Him with song and with action, and we tell others about Him.

In this way, looking forward to the source of our faith, we run and we yell because we are free.

READ COLOSSIANS 2:20-23. Rewrite the question in verse 20 in your own words.

....

....

Paul writes to those who have been trying to live by man made rules and regulations. Despite the fact that these laws and rules were not given by God, people still worked to keep them. Paul asks a simple question, *If you are a new creation in Jesus, why do you live like you are still trapped?*

If you are a believer, in what ways do you find yourself still living as one who still belongs to the world?

....

....

What rules and regulations imposed by yourself or others would you need to let go in order to live as a new creation?

....

....

Read the following verses, noting what each one says about life as a new creation in Christ:

Colossians 3:1-17

....

....

Romans 6:1-15

....

....

2 Corinthians 4:14-18

....

....

2 Peter 1:4-8

....

....

You have been set free! You can run and leap and yell because sin no longer has a hold on you—you've thrown it off. You've renewed your mind, tearing down the walls and the chains and the lies. You've put on truth and running shoes. Now run toward Jesus.

DAY 2

Write It Down

I can't even begin to count the times I've thought, I don't need to write that down—I'll remember! And then later realize my memory skills are not the best. I have trouble with a simple grocery list sometimes, so trying to remember how I felt in a situation or what I thought at a certain time can be difficult.

I now try to live by the rule: Always write it down.

The same holds true for our change process.

Change takes work, time, and perseverance. Even when we know the path to freedom, running down it requires training. We don't simply decide one day, "Today I am going to start thinking about what is true!"

Like in everything, practice helps. We can begin to practice transformation in our lives by writing things down.

Would you consider yourself a journaler?

....

You may have answered no and I completely understand. However, I would encourage you to start one. If the blank page scares you a little, don't worry. Today we're going to explore what a change-practice journal entry looks like.

In bold, you'll find questions to ask yourself when tempted. I'll explain a little about each one, but the bolded questions will help you direct your journaling so that you can remember later. In remembering, we celebrate what God has done and we learn to watch for certain triggers and pitfalls we may encounter in the future. If you've already learned "a way out" of temptation (1 Corinthians 10:13), there's no reason to forge a new path—go out the same way next time!

In answering all of these questions, be honest. The only people reading it are you and God.

In what way was I tempted?

Be as specific as possible.

....

....

What lie did I tell myself?

An example of the lie might be: "If I worry about this situation, I have control over it." Often, the lie may seem ridiculous at first, but ignore that. Write down whatever it was that you believed would be true if you gave into temptation.

....

....

What does God say about this lie?

This is where you'll need your Bible. Find what God's Word says about your lie. Find out what He says about control, about honoring your body, about trying to be perfect, about comparison. Write it down in full here.

....

....

....

....

What is true, lovely, and praiseworthy?

Your answer here may or may not be the same as the one above. Maybe you wrote above a command not to do a certain thing. Here, write what is true about God, about you, about the world. In the example of worry, I might write down verses about God's sovereignty, about fear, and about trusting Him here.

....

....

If you see the same verse appear day after day in this section, commit it to memory. Write it down and stick it on your mirror, your dashboard, your refrigerator, your computer.

What do I need to repent of?

Pray asking for forgiveness for any sin you may have committed.

....

What actions can I take to put others first and give God the glory?

Name one person you can help in some way today. Make a plan to serve and love that person (and others you may encounter).

....

....

What am I thankful for?

Make a new list here or add to the list you made last week. Read over the other items, thanking God for each of them.

....

....

....

....

Pray.

Thank God for His Word. Thank Him for giving us what is true, lovely, praiseworthy. Ask forgiveness for disobeying Him. Ask for help in turning from temptation. Thank Him for always providing a way out. Thank Him for hope.

You'll notice at first that you journal often as you practice applying the three steps to your life. As you practice more and more, though, you'll learn to do the process without writing it down. You'll memorize Scripture and your response time will get faster and faster. I'm praying that for you.

―――― **DAY 3** ――――

Tell of This

Whenever I find something helpful in life—whether it is a truth in Scripture or something as silly as a funny meme online that made me laugh—I share it. I want my friends to be included in the knowledge I've obtained. I want to share it with them so that they, too, can experience what I did. I also want to include others so we can celebrate together. I'm an introvert, but I still believed shared experiences are the most rich experiences.

We've been on a journey here. We've learned what it means to be wonder-fully made in His image. We walked through the entrance of sin and shame into our paradise. We praised Jesus for the covering of His blood over us, for making us new creations. We learned the steps of the journey toward freedom and truth and we practiced walking it. We watched our chains loosen and fall as we began, perhaps for the first time, to look toward Jesus and start running.

READ 2 CORINTHIANS 1:3-8. What do these verses tell you about our suffering?

....

....

When we suffer, we are able to turn and comfort others who are suffering. Think about that. How powerful is it to hear someone tell their story and think, "This is exactly what I'm going through"? We have that in Jesus, our high priest, and we also have that in other believers.

Can you think of someone who has suffered in the same way you have? How did their comfort overflow to you?

....

....

How can the comfort you've found in Scripture comfort other people?

....

....

We can't keep this goodness to ourselves!

Read Psalm 107:1-2:

Give thanks to the LORD, for he is good;
his faithful love endures forever.
Let the redeemed of the LORD proclaim
that he has redeemed them from the power of the foe

What does *redeem* mean? Use your dictionary if you need it!

....

We give thanks for redemption, but it doesn't stop there. Let the redeemed of the Lord proclaim.

When I think of the word proclaim I think of royal proclamations—someone standing on a cobblestone path reading a scroll to a rapt audience. We should be so excited to tell what God has done for us!

Throughout the psalms, we see similar declarations. When God's people think of the ways He has delivered and redeemed them, they can't help but tell others.

READ MATTHEW 28:18:20. What are we commanded to do?

....

....

If we follow Jesus, we tell others about Him. We not only tell about Him, but we walk beside others as they go on the same journey we've walked. Their temptations may be different, but we all search for freedom from sin and lies. When Jesus tells us to make disciples, He commands us to teach others how to live. Teach them to observe His commands—to throw off our sin, to renew our minds, and to dwell on what is true.

Think about the people you know. Who needs to hear this news? Write their names here and pray for an opportunity to share with them. Pray also for boldness to do so.

....

....

Friend, let's proclaim how God has redeemed us. Let's yell it!

DAY 4

On our last day of study together, I want to do something a little different. Today, instead of journaling (since we did that on Day 2), let's read and meditate on a portion of Colossians 1. This part of Scripture makes me want to laugh and cry and yell all at the same time because God is so good to us! Pray this Scripture, asking for it to be true of you, thanking Jesus for who He is and what He's done.

9 For this reason also, since the day we heard this, we haven't stopped praying for you. We are asking that you may be filled with the knowledge of his will in all wisdom and spiritual understanding,

10 so that you may walk worthy of the Lord, fully pleasing to him: bearing fruit in every good work and growing in the knowledge of God,

11 being strengthened with all power, according to his glorious might, so that you may have great endurance and patience, joyfully

12 giving thanks to the Father, who has enabled you to share in the saints' inheritance in the light.

13 He has rescued us from the domain of darkness and transferred us into the kingdom of the Son he loves.

14 In him we have redemption, the forgiveness of sins.

15
He is the image of the invisible God,
the firstborn over all creation.

16
For everything was created by him,
in heaven and on earth,
the visible and the invisible,
whether thrones or dominions
or rulers or authorities—
all things have been created through him and for him.

17
He is before all things,
and by him all things hold together.

18
He is also the head of the body, the church;
he is the beginning,
the firstborn from the dead,
so that he might come to have
first place in everything.

19
For God was pleased to have
all his fullness dwell in him,

20
and through him to reconcile
everything to himself,
whether things on earth or things in heaven,
by making peace
through his blood, shed on the cross.

21   Once you were alienated and hostile in your minds expressed in your evil actions.

22   But now he has reconciled you by his physical body through his death, to present you holy, faultless, and blameless before him—

23   if indeed you remain grounded and steadfast in the faith and are not shifted away from the hope of the gospel that you heard. This gospel has been proclaimed in all creation under heaven, and I, Paul, have become a servant of it.

May the same
be true of us.

Amen.

Week 8

VIDEO TIME

REVIEW QUESTIONS:

1. Practically, what does it look like in your life to keep your eyes on Christ?

....

....

2. What does it look like to live as a new creation?

....

....

3. Have you had a chance to use your journal questions yet? If so, share something you learned from doing so (you don't have to share all your answers).

....

....

4. What have you been so excited about you couldn't wait to tell everyone you know?

....

....

5. What is most challenging to you about telling of the redemption of the Lord?

....

....

WATCH THE VIDEO TEACHING.

VIDEO QUESTIONS:

1. Read Ephesians 6:18-20 together. Why is prayer important as a weapon against the lies of the enemy?

....

....

2. Pray for one another, that you can stand strong in the truths you've learned. Pray that you will be able to encourage one another in the coming days, weeks, months, and years.

You're rooted. You're equipped. You're ready. We can't wait to see how God uses your freedom for your glory and His good.

This week's Next Right Step from our friends at FINDING*balance*®:

Get – and STAY – connected! The work God is doing in you can continue as you engage with others who are seeking God's freedom from food and body image issues. If you haven't already connected with our friends at FINDING*balance*, take a moment to check out the great support groups and other resources they have for you at www.findingbalance.com/freedom

NEED SUPPORT TODAY?

To find Christ-centered support and resources to help you repair your relationship with food and your body, visit our friends at FINDING*balance*, a 501(c)(3) nonprofit est. 2002.

www.findingbalance.com/freedom

To find out more about Alyssa Bethke head over to:

🌐 www.jeffandalyssa.com

📷 instagram.com/alyssajoybethke

f www.facebook.com/alyssajoybethke/

To Find out more about Sadie Robertson head over to:

🌐 www.liveoriginal.com

📷 instagram.com/legisadierob

f www.facebook.com/sadiecrobertson

YOU LOVE JESUS BUT
LIFE STILL HURTS

Power of The Psalms is an online video course with Alyssa Bethke. It's easy to understand yet goes deep, and will help you read the psalms with more clarity, excitement, and freshness as well is show you how they can meet you in your deepest need and hurt.

www.powerofthepsalms.com

Dr. Susan Peirce Thompson has created a simple and highly effective quiz that will help you discover how susceptible you are to the addictive properties of refined foods.

Upon completing the quiz, you will receive your score and a personalized video from **Dr. Susan Peirce Thompson** regarding your uniquesusceptibility profile and key research findings on the Brain Science of Sustainable Weight Loss.

Start the quiz here:

www.findingfreedomworkshop.com/quiz

Made in USA - Kendallville, IN
1162603_9781734274660